The Spirit of the Bush

and other verse

'The Larrikin'
Bruce Venables

RANDOM HOUSE AUSTRALIA

Random House Australia Pty Ltd
20 Alfred Street, Milsons Point, NSW 2061
http://www.randomhouse.com.au

Sydney   New York   Toronto
London   Auckland   Johannesburg

First published by Random House Australia 2003

National Library of Australia
Cataloguing-in-Publication Entry

Venables, Bruce.
Spirit of the bush.

ISBN 1 74051 251 0

I. Title
A821.3

Cover illustration by Bill Leak
Internal illustrations by Warren Brown
Cover design by Darian Causby/Highway 51
Typeset in 11/14 Bembo by Midland Typesetters, Maryborough, Victoria
Printed and bound by Griffin Press, Netley, South Australia

10   9   8   7   6   5   4   3   2   1

This book is dedicated to
my mother, Molly Venables

And in loving memory of
my father, Norman,
and
my brother, Ross

Contents

Preface

I have my mother, Molly, to thank for my love of literature. When I was only two years old I was badly burned in a gas fire and was unable to walk for several years. The resulting scars to my legs made me a solitary little boy and I avoided the company of other children. The pain and trauma the incident obviously brought with it has blocked out any memory I have of the first five or six years of my childhood, except for the face of my mother, Molly Venables, and the deep and abiding love she surrounded me with. I truly believe that without this love and the love shown to me by my father, Norman Sydney Venables, and Ross, my only brother, older than me by five years, I would not have survived the obstacle course of youth.

My first pictorial memory is of a wooden bookcase, built for me in school wood-working class by Ross. It sat on the mantelpiece in our bedroom and my mother filled it with the twelve volumes of *Arthur Mee's Children's Encyclopedia*. This was at great cost and sacrifice, because the encyclopedias were very expensive. By the time I was ten years old I'd read these books from cover to cover and my thirst for reading was insatiable. My mother continued to supply the books and I continued just as rapidly to devour them, but supply was always outstripped by demand. As a consequence I read my mother's library books and anything else I found lying around the house, which ran the gamut of authors, from Sir Richard Burton, James Joyce, Frank Harris, Fyodor Dostoyevsky, Aleksandr Solzhenitsyn, Henry Miller and Anais Nin, to Sir Arthur Conan Doyle, J.M. Barrie, Enid Blyton and the romance novels of Jean Plaidy. Needless to say I became a very confused boy!

Enter my father, Norm, into the bizarre world of my formative education. My father was not a reader – in fact the only books he every read, by his own admission, were Australian bush verse collections he carried around with him during the Depression while jumping trains to look for work. Whenever he sensed I was down or unhappy, he'd rattle off a verse or two by Paterson, Lawson, Ogilvie or Kendall and so, from him, I learned to love the galloping metre and rhyme that typified the rhythms and patterns of Australian speech. I must say my father never knew a complete poem and when I asked him why, he simply replied, 'I only memorised the good bits', which, when you think about it, is a remark steeped in wisdom. My mother soon realised a good book of Aussie verse would shut me up for a month so she lavished them upon me. You therefore have my loving family to thank for what you are about to be subjected to.

I am very proud to be an Australian and I love my country dearly. I love the wild, anti-authority spirit it has bred in us and I love the fact that part of my heritage is the oldest surviving culture of them all, the Dreamtime. There is a reckless spirit or a touch of the larrikin in all Australians, no matter what our antecedents or ethnic backgrounds, and it is this larrikinism I love above all. I'm proud to be a larrikin, a person who can do or say whatever he bloody well likes, whenever and wherever he bloody well pleases as long as he remains within the laws of his society. So embrace the doctrine, be a larrikin, it is your inalienable right as an Australian.

'The Larrikin', Bruce Venables
Sydney
7 March 2003

About Bill Leak and Warren Brown

Bill Leak is a larrikin of the first water! I know this to be a fact because he is my friend. He is one of the finest artists Australia has ever produced as well as the brilliant cartoonist for *The Australian*. He also loves a chat. He was on air recently in a regular late-night radio spot on the ABC, which nobody listened to, and do you think that shut him up? No! His larrikin spirit rose above the fact that he was talking to the ether and he said what had to be said! Whatever that was.

I walked into the National Portrait Gallery recently for the opening of Barry Humphries' exhibition and the first thing to confront me was a portrait of Robert Hughes painted by Bill Leak. I had not seen the portrait for some time and I was physically shocked by the power of it. I stood there for a full minute, and in that minute I lived the life of Robert Hughes. I felt his pain, his anguish, his loss, his arrogance, his love, his compassion and his triumph. Bill had captured it all with a brush and some paint and I was in awe of his accomplishment.

Bill Leak's a good man. For many people, a modicum of talent goes hand in hand with insufferable arrogance, but with great talent there is usually humility. This is the case with Leak: he is genuinely humble about his work and would never bask in the sunshine that sycophants (and they abound in the art world) desire to bathe him in. The knockabout, larrikin attitude he exudes is not a pretence, it is very real, and for that I truly admire him. He'll cringe if he ever reads this, but I believe he should be declared a national treasure, taken to Canberra and put in a box for safe-keeping.

To anyone who ever listened to the 'Goon Show' on radio, Warren Brown is Neddy Seagoon born into another life, and in his next life he'll be reborn as Bluebottle. Warren is the wonderful child in us all and he is the brilliant cartoonist who reflects the rhythms and moods of the Harbour City in his cartoons for the *Daily Telegraph*. Like any person with a great talent, he has an unassuming nature and a genuine modesty about his achievements. I know him as a friend, a wonderfully warm-hearted and compassionate man who would give you the shirt off his back, provided you helped him undo the buttons. Whenever I think of Warren Brown, I am reminded of summer holidays by the beach, trout fishing in the Shannon River and hundreds and thousands on bread and butter.

Blessed with an inexhaustible supply of good humour and a creative aptitude shared by very few, Warren is ever ready to help out, no matter what the cause, and he once played a song for me on his banjo when I was unhappy. It is my considered opinion that Brown has done for country music what Stonehenge did for rocks. Furthermore, he genuinely means it when he tells you that his favourite song is 'Gunfight at the O.K. Corral' by Marty Robbins and that he goes to Gowings to get his hair cut. There is an ineffable honesty about him that shines like the brightest star in a night sky and a generosity of spirit that knows no bounds. He is a remarkable fellow, a fine artist, a true larrikin and a person I'm proud to call my friend.

Australiana

G'day

Came the Dreamtime, came the Black Man, came the Serpent, came
    the Dingo
Came the Tears down from the Moon to give the Life.
Came the Emu, Kookaburra, came the Love for one another,
Came the White Man, came the Heartbreak, came the Strife.

Came the Sunshine, came the Harvest, came the Nation, came the Battle
Came the Famine, came another world-wide war.
Came the Migrants, came the Good Life, came the Power, came the Present.
Come the Treaty. Unity for ever more.

So here we are in the two thousands and there's more of us than cows
And over half of us have come from foreign lands.
Jews and Christians, Buddhists, Muslims, Bondi sheilas with big bosoms
And there's still one mob or two don't understand.

Multiculture as a standard means you must be even-handed
Say g'day and give a bloke a go.
You can lend him your lawn mower, if you think that he's a goer
And if you really truly like him let him know.

Ask him where he used to come from, before he was an Aussie
Fill your head with knowledge from his side.
Get to know him like a brother, till you're used to one another
And you'll find you'll start to feel good, deep inside.

Have him over on a Sunday, sit and watch as all the kids play
'Cause they're the answer to the game, you see?
They don't know the past from Adam, knew no Hitler, Stalin, Saddam
As far as they're concerned their world is free.

But make sure in what you're doing, that those kids know what to do
In times when Hatred raises its great head.
Tell them stories of the Anzacs and of Auschwitz and the Race Acts
Say the Age of Evil Deeds is never dead.

Tell them, always keep a vigil, or the ghosts of Lone Pine Ridge will
Come to haunt them in the hour before the dawn.
We must keep the watchfire burning as the years keep slowly turning
'Lest We Forget' and darkness be reborn.

Tell your kids they share a great land, nurtured by the mighty Koori
And the Dreamtime is our true Eternal Flame.
Tell them thanks for all the wonders, in this wonderland Down Under
And say 'sorry that we once denied your name'.

Keep the billabongs and ridges far removed from kitchen fridges
Use the power of the wind to light your way.
Guard the land with all your passion, make things plastic out of fashion,
Let the healing powers of Nature have their way.

Share this land with all who dwell here, let the world know we are
        well here
In this place of promise and diversity.
Shout 'g'day' and 'howyagoin' 'neath our flag that's proudly blowing
O'er this land of peace and love and liberty.

A Senior Australian

Delivered at the Senior Australian of the Year Award 2000

I'm a senior Australian. What's that you say?
My waistline is thicker and my hair has turned grey.
How very observant, it happens with time
You learn to accept it, when you pass your prime.

That's prime of the body, not of the mind
I'm still very able, not deaf, dumb and blind.
In fact I'm quite active, yes, sexually too
Forgive me, you've gone red. Did I upset you?

I find that I do that so often these days
Upset you young people with things that I say.
It isn't deliberate, I don't mean to be short
It's all of the angst and the battles I've fought.

Yes! Yes, I know, you've got battles to fight
I know how you're feeling. You're probably right.
Yes! Yes, I know that you must make your stand
But please don't presume that I don't understand.

Change is required. I hear what you say
To hell with the old guard, each dog has its day.
Vive la revolution! Stand tall in the sun!
What's that you say? You are buying a gun?

Will you listen a moment? Indulge an old fool
It's been many years now since I went to school.
The School of Hard Knocks. Please, don't raise your eyes
It's one thing in the young that I really despise.

The School of Hard Knocks is a lifetime affair
You don't graduate till there's grey in your hair.
There is no diploma, no cap and no gown
You just learn to get up every time you're knocked down.

Silence! Don't say it, not even a word
If you're buying a gun, I've the right to be heard.
If there's one thing I learned in the School of Hard Knocks
It's if you buy a gun, you end up in a box.

Come back here this instant! How dare you walk out!
I bloody well know what I'm talking about!
You see? At my age the passion's still there
Yes I'll calm down, if you'll pull up a chair.

Come on, sit down. Life will wait for one day
I think it's important, what I have to say.
Please stay a while and listen to me
Why don't I make us a nice cup of tea?

Owning a gun is an adult decision
But people my age view guns with derision.
I'm sure with your peers, the decision's correct
But then there's the Law of Cause and Effect.

What does it mean? Cause and Effect?
I'm not really sure, it's rather complex.
It's to do with Nature and the scheme of things
Ever opened your mouth and heard someone else sing?

What? How could I have an effect on your bowel?
I can't even correct the sound of your vowels.
All right! Okay! I'll be serious
But let's spend some time. Just the two of us.

My dad, your grandad, fought in the war
He was killed in the islands, nineteen forty-four
And your great grandad fought at the Somme in 'sixteen
They say it's the worst war the world's ever seen.

Your uncles fought in a war as well
They both said Vietnam was worse than hell.
Your own brother David went off to Iraq
I was so terrified that he wouldn't come back.

They talked of strange places when they returned
Of battlefields distant and cities that burned.
Where they buried their mates just as the sun set
They still whisper those place names, lest we forget.

You've read those names when you've passed the shrines
Long Tan and Tobruk, The Nek and Lone Pine.
Kokoda, Beersheba, Korea, Alamein
Where young men lie sleeping and nothing was gained.

You see what I'm saying? A nod will do
If you buy a gun you'll go off to war too.
Take it from me, I've lived through it, kid
And I've had to live with the things those wars did.

They solved bloody nothing! Except World War Two
Hitler was no good. That everyone knew
But as for the others I'm telling you, son
They all came from young blokes like you buying guns.

I'm glad that we're having a chat like this
Because it's quite true that a gap can exist.
Between you young and the older, like me
It's good that we're talking, here have some more tea.

Sorry, what's that? You're enjoying the chat?
Yes, there is some knowledge under this hat.
And you know of things I don't understand
Like Internet stuff and clocks without hands.

You can tell me of what it is like to be young
Your songs are different to the ones that I sung.
Do you find that time passes too slowly for you?
I remember when it went too slow for me too.

I've noticed your friends are a fairly mixed lot
All types and colours, a real melting pot.
That's the way things are going, and not before time
What went on in my day was simply a crime.

Multiculture is something I'm trying to grasp
And I know it's important so I'm learning fast.
My new neighbour's an Aboriginal bloke
And yesterday we finally spoke.

His name is Alf and his wife's called Shirl
They've got a beaut little boy and a beaut little girl.
You'll never guess what I went and did
I gave your old bike away to his kids.

If we talk together then problems get solved
You're young, you see, and full of resolve.
But I'm older and wiser and make no mistake
The getting of wisdom's one thing you can't fake.

The School of Hard Knocks, yes, go on and smile
Yet I could beat you by a country mile.
Not at running or jumping – you'd beat me with ease
But at planning a future where the world is at peace.

History's mistakes are what I have here
Up in my head. And they're so crystal clear.
Written as memories with Age as the pen
Don't buy a gun and commit them again.

The choice is yours. I make no demand
You can dismiss me with a wave of your hand.
Ignore me, deride me, call me an alien
Or you can listen and learn from a senior Australian.

The Great Hall, Parliament House
Canberra
4 October 2000

The Poppies of Phillip Island

West wind from Bass Strait increases
The last light has died in the west
Night falls upon Phillip Island
Wildlife seek shelter and rest.

The rise of the wind on the water
Confuses the black angry sea
Where fishing boats nod in the darkness;
Old soldiers with sad memories.

White heat of the day is relentless
Blue warmth of the evening's divine
The Summer Moon shines through a halo
Like the glow of a lamp through red wine.

In the tavern a Monet is hanging
A print that has seen better days
It depicts a field full of red poppies
And a mother and daughter at play.

The wind in the pine trees is moaning
It whispers through dark chicory
It calls to the Muse of the dancing
The raven-haired Terpsichore.

The sound of flamenco in courtyards
The thud of a heel upon stone
The clap of a call to a lover
No one is left standing alone.

The Muse sets the night air to rhythm
The fingers on strings play her tune
The tempo builds in a crescendo
Frightening the clouds from the Moon.

On a table stand *cuatro floreros*
Their prisoners, four poppies red
Amapolas de la Isla Felipe
They plead with the Moon overhead.

The Moon calls the Muse to her station
A whispered command is soon passed
The Muse, laughing, suddenly orders
Each poppy released from its vase.

On a sudden four raven-haired beauties
Stand proud in a frozen tableau
Arms stretching high, fingers curling
Atop the *mantillas* and bows.

The revellers are transfixed in wonder
As onto the dance floor they flow
A passionate strum on the guitar
Bids them spin into wild flamenco.

With the clip-clap-clap and the rat-tat-tat
Of the feet and the hands and the castanets
And the swirl of the dresses and the sensual caresses
Of the fingers on the throat and the breast

And the hands they dance in a shared romance
Come one, come the other, then entwined in one another
And the dancers glance as they stamp and prance
Till they take their chance with a last advance
Rushing with the music to a high-armed stance then they freeze!

In silence they stand there majestic
Beads of sweat running down onto breasts
Heaving wildly till Passion escapes them
Then they sway to their table and rest.

'Neath the lanterns some semblance of order
Replaces the fanciful flight
And the people all gather in clusters
Bidding each other goodnight.

The barman rings his *campanilla*
The players pack up their guitars
The old men head off for the river
To drink wine and smoke their cigars.

The revellers stroll off in the moonlight
Musicians walk home to their wives
All aware that for one shining moment
Enchantment had entered their lives.

On the table the empty *floreros*
Hear the Muse lull the beauties to sleep
And morning will find them returned to
Amapolas de la Isla Felipe.

Australia Day 2001

Australia Day Ambassador Speech, Eurobodalla Shire, 2001

A man flew into Sydney from some far off foreign country
And approached an Aussie standing by the sea
'I'm on a search for Freedom, it is somewhere in this world
'I wondered if you know where it might be?

'I've heard of its existence and I need to find it badly
'My legs are weary and my heart is sad
'My family is home weeping for our future's disappeared
'The country that we live in has gone mad.

'I'm accused because I'm faithful to the God that I love dearly
'And abused over the colour of my wife
'My children have no schooling and my country's run by tyrants
'And if I do not obey I'll lose my life.

'Tell me is it that way here? Do dogs of war harass you?
'Or is the tide of Freedom on the flood?
'Do you walk the earth so free because your family has money?
'Or perhaps it is that you're of royal blood?'

'Nah, my mother was a Koori,' said the Aussie with a smile
'And my father he was Irish from the South
'And his father was part Indian and his wife was Portuguese
'Mum says that's where I get my sensual mouth.

'And my mother's gran was English, or so it was she claimed
'But I think she had a touch of something else
'She was born of Slav and Russian stock, or so my uncle said
'Mind you, he spoke authentic Welsh.

'You ought to see my sister, she's as black as ebony
'And my other sister's sort of Chinese gold
'But they look the same as I do when they're in a softer light
'Like my cousins down in Adelaide, so I'm told.

'See this amulet I'm wearing that means I am part Hindu
'This yamulka that I wear means I'm part Jew
'And I've got a bit of Muslim in me on my grandad's side
'But my religion is the Dreamtime point of view.

'You wouldn't know the Dreamtime seeing you're from far away
'Its philosophy is older than the sun
'It is spoken by the "First Ones", they're the tribes who've lived
        "Down Under"
'Ever since The Time of Man begun.

'They call it Alcheringa, when the world was just a dream
'And all the things in nature came to be
'And Man was made the guardian of all of Nature's wonders
'See, philosophy like that appeals to me.

'But my nephew follows Islam and my niece is Protestant
'And my Aunty Elsie is a Buddhist nun
'In fact, all my family's different, we've just got one thing in common
'And that is we are all Australian.

'Cross-bred I am, you might say, and you wouldn't be far wrong
'A mongrel through and through I s'pose you'd say
'I've got German blood, Iraqi and some Greek–Italian too
'And some Lebanese got in along the way.

'When you add a dash of Swedish, then some Polish and some Serb
'My antecedents may sound rather mucky
'But then you're not from Australia so you wouldn't understand
'If I told you that I think I'm bloody lucky.

'To you a mongrel is a cur, a cross-bred dog not worth its fur
'Here Down Under that idea's been turned about
'We have known the world at war and seen the racial hatred
'So we integrate to stamp that nonsense out.

'We're a nation of all races, smiling eyes and friendly faces
'And above all we're a nation that is free
'If people tell us what to do, or how to act, or what to say
'We tell them all to go to buggery.

'I don't know where you call home,' said the Aussie to the stranger
'But it doesn't sound too free where you come from.'
'I'm sad to say it isn't,' said the stranger with a sigh
'And my country's full of unexploded bombs.

'But one day I will return here to your land of kangaroos
'And boomerangs and Dreamtime harmony
'I like the sort of place where there is one collective race
'And next time I will bring my family.

'I'll tell all of my children of your story of the "First Ones"
'And we will help preserve this wide brown land
'And when I do return is there a chance you might be waiting
'To give my family a helping hand?'

'Now that would be a privilege,' said the Aussie to the stranger
'Let me know and I'll be at the airport gate
'And when you get off that plane with your wife and kids in train
'I'll shake your hand and say good on ya, mate!

'And when you take the oath of allegiance to this country
'And recognise it as your sovereign nation
'I'll take your hand so proudly and I'll shout out bloody loudly
'"Welcome to our land! Congratulations."'

The Bush

Emu Bush –
on the road to Goodooga...

WARREN

The Spirit of the Bush

There's trouble out there as I speak, made up of wind and dust
It howls around the homesteads and the rain tanks, gone to rust
The animals are dying, all choked up with flies and sand
And though country folks aren't saying much, they need a helping hand.

They're hard as nails those bushmen, but this time they're on their knees
This drought has got them to the stage where they're in dire need
But they're not beg-or-borrow-folk, and they don't cheat or lie
They'll do it hard in silence and I'm here to tell you why.

There's a pulse that beats in the bush country beyond the Great Divide
You can feel it from the Snowies for as far as you can ride
You can sense it when you see the brush of breezes on the rivers
It'll touch your soul where e'er you go and cause your spine to shiver.

Born of the men who worked the land on outback cattle stations
In the olden days when times were hard at the birth of our great nation
It's a melding of the Dreamtime with the heart of Never-Never
That then blended with the souls who came here after Cook's endeavour.

It's a force made up of all that's fair and noble in the bush
It's the strength that makes an Aussie bushie give it 'one more push'
It's the decency that makes a person lend a helping hand
It's the valour shown at Lone Pine and Kakoda and Long Tan.

In the bush they call it being 'dinkum', 'straight up', or 'true blue'
They don't discuss it often, it's just something that they do
It's the mateship that'll help the bloke who's broke or down and out
It's the guts it takes to fight the bloody bushfires and the drought.

You watch how fast they go to work when Nature takes a turn
When raging floods strike dingo-like or roaring bushfires burn
Or when a screaming cyclone flattens half a dozen towns
Watch how quick those country hearts will help those who are down.

That's the spirit, don't you see, that gives the bush its power?
The people stick and do it tough all through the darkest hour
No one shirks or backs away, it's 'Shoulders to the wheel!'
That's the spirit of the bush, old mate, and that's the pulse you feel.

So spare a thought next time you're driving down a country road
For all those sunburnt people out there carrying the load
Stop and listen for a second and I'll bet your pulse starts racing
That's the spirit of the bush my friend, the heartland of our nation.

Enough

Let me tell you stranger, don't be fooled by all this rain
My farm will not recover. Ten years' work's gone down the drain.

The trouble isn't over just because it's pissing down
At the moment it's forgotten 'cause there's flash floods in the town.

There's water for the livestock and some crops will start to shoot
But in a week or so you're gonna need your desert boots.

It's gonna take five years for me to get back on the square
And then there'll be another drought! I'll tell you, it's not fair!

Up the creek without a paddle I am, you might say
But what's the good of paddling, there's no water anyway!

There's a lot of good men leaving, they're just walking off the land
Land, did I say? Jesus Christ! It's more like bloody sand!

This bloody drought's the worst I've known in forty bloody years
My kid's are feeling guilty and my missus is in tears.

And none of this is their fault, it's just nature at its worst
The rain could go on pissing down. It wouldn't be a first.

Next thing the bloody stock'll drown and then the dams'll burst
Aah, bugger it! I've had enough! By Christ I've got a thirst.

You fancy going to the pub? I'd love a beer all right!
If I go home I'll just stare at the ceiling through the night.

I know the kids aren't sleeping, they're all staring up there too
Sick worrying about their mum and what their dad will do.

I don't know what I'm gonna do, I don't know where to turn
I suppose I'll end up in the city looking for an earn.

I've got to face the fact that Mother Nature's called my bluff
The stakes are just too bloody high, and I have had enough!

Water Down Under

Dedicated to Steve Mason

I was out the back of nowhere leaning on a stockyard fence
When a bloke from back of Bourke gave me a drink
Which I gratefully accepted then remarked that it was dry
And he said, 'It's not as dry as you might think.

'There's water all around us here, but you won't see a drop,'
Laughed this bushman from the Darling's western side.
'It's up in half of Queensland and the Territory too
'You'll find it for as far as you can ride.

'Even down in South Australia if you care to take a look
'You'll find it in the far north-eastern bit.
'Mate, a quarter of this country's fairly rotten with the stuff.
'God's truth! You're standing right on top of it.

'It's called artesian water 'cause it's underneath the ground.
'The Great Artesian Basin is its name.
'It's been abused for bloody years by every Tom and Dick and Harry
'Until now it has become a national shame.

'Way back in the eighteen seventies the bastards first discovered
'That if you sunk a bore into the earth,
'The source of life came flying through the pipe up to the surface
'And shot into the air for all it's worth.

'I can see the fools all dancing round and hugging one another
'As the water spilled about them on the ground.
'Falling to their bloody knees and sending thankyou up to Jesus
'While the water was just wasting all around.

'But the bastards didn't cap them! They just let those wells keep gushing
'Till the country was a mass of man-made lakes
'With the stock just wading through it. Never thinking for a minute
'That near ninety-five per cent evaporates.

'Fifteen hundred wells were drilled by nineteen hundred ten
'All uncapped and fairly spewing water out.
'What a crying waste it was of one of Nature's precious bounties
'Until finally the bores just wouldn't spout.

'When they realised they'd lost pressure then they started using pumps
'So's to suck the water clear up to the rim.
'Even then they never capped them! They just left the water running!
'It's prob'ly where they taught their kids to swim.

'The worst crime was the governments of the day did bloody nothing
'And successive governments have done the same.
'They could've drought-proofed the whole country then, for
        damn posterity
'But posterity to pollies is a game.

'A game of hanging in there for a parliamentary pension
'While avoiding the real questions of the day.
'They could have sorted all this out over a hundred years ago
'If they'd let the visionaries have their way.

'Parliamentary visionaries? That's a dead-set oxymoron
'Politicians with the brains to see and think?
'They're all fools! They're just like horses, you can lead them both to water
'But you try getting either one to drink.

'Five thousand bores were sunk, over the years, across the Basin
'But no one's ever dared enforce the law
'Made by fifties legislation that says all bores must be capped
''Cause in fifty years they've capped just one in four.

'If only someone had the guts to cap the bores and pipe the water
'Way down under where it won't evaporate,
'To the east of where I'm standing would be bulletproof from drought
'But pretty soon it's gonna be too late.

'I tell pollies, if the bores were capped and usage was restricted
'There'd be water for emergencies and such,
'Like the killing times of bushfires and the hard times of the droughts
'But they just say that it'd cost too much.'

'I wonder if they'll say that now that Canberra's burnt to cinders?
'Maybe that'll stop them buying air force jets.
'You know the price of one war plane could set this country up forever?
'That has got to be as stupid as it gets!

'It's the irrigators too, the neo-bastards of the bush
'They're choking off the rivers running south.
'Making millions with the water that they leave unfit to drink!
'When you taste it, it's like cotton in your mouth.

'There are some say it's sustainable, that's scientific gabble
'Supposed to mean the G.A.B. will flow forever,
'But they're public servant boffins, they know what side their bread
        is buttered.
'The truth's out here beneath the Never-Never.

'Way out here they tell it different, they believe the Basin's dying
'But there's no one who will listen to their tale.
'Underground they say it's struggling, 'cause it's not being replenished
'And the truth is that one day it's gonna fail!

'The Great Australian Basin! It could make Australia healthy
'For forever and forever, say amen.
'But if you think we can abuse it for forever and forever,
'You'd be wise to take a drink, and think again.'

West of Bourke
February 2003

The Old Stone Fence

'Built by convicts,' the old man said
'Long afore my time.
'It was there when my old dad was a boy
'And the land was in its prime.

'The bit on the end was added on
'When me uncle came home from the war.
'He built another bit down by the creek
'But he never said what for.

'He was at the Somme when they turned it on,
'I think 'e got knocked in the 'ead.'
The old man emptied his pipe on the gate.
'He couldn't forget all the dead.

'He drowned you know, in that dam down there
'In the flood of twenty-four.
'Truth of it was 'e killed 'isself,
'He couldn't go on any more.

'He used to say each stone in the fence
'Was the soul of a man that fell.
'My uncle had a haunted look
'Like a bloke who'd been to hell.

'Terrible lot of them died, you know,
'Ten thousand or more they say.
'All because some toff got shot.
'It's a terrible price to pay.

'They thought it was right to go to war,
'King and Country and such.
'But lookin' back on it all from 'ere,
'It didn't amount to much.

'Bloody silly, war, you know,
'No one ever wins.
'Men fight and die and twenty years on
'Their sons repeat their sins.

'The priest! I 'eard 'im sayin' that
'In the pub the other night.
'Snowy said, "S'all right for you,
Your lot don't have to fight."

'Drunk 'e was, just mouthin' off.
'Son in Vietnam.
'The publican said 'e'd offended the priest,
'But Snow didn't give a damn.

'There's lots like Snow. Bitter, you know?
'It's the talk that does the harm.
'I keep well away from that sorta stuff.
'Spend most of my time on the farm.

'I can't understand what gets into men
'Like Snowy and those of his ilk.'
He stared out over the low-lying hills,
Then sighed, 'I got cows to milk.'

In the gathering dusk I watched him go
Through the shadows from off the shed.
And all of a sudden, in No-Man's Land
I stood with the souls of the dead.

The Vision Splendid

'He sees the vision splendid,' said a man who once extended
A hand out to his rough-house countrymen
And his words should still ring true to all Aussies old and new
For not that much has changed since way back then.

And what has changed is for the better since the Banjo wrote that letter
Which was answered 'with a thumbnail dipped in tar'
In these days of blood and thunder there's no need for us to wonder
We Down Under know exactly where we are.

We're in the mighty Southern Ocean and we've set some things
        in motion
That will see us marching to a different drum
A fine republic's what I see with a people proud and free
Who will show this troubled world just how it's done.

I can see that 'vision splendid of the sunlit plains extended'
Can you see it? Oh I really hope you do
Filled with smiling Aussie faces fused from oh, so many races
Left to them in trust by me and you.

And in the in-between time we must tell them of the Dreamtime
World of Koori peace and harmony
So they nurture this great land, passing it from hand to hand
Preserving it all for posterity.

Can you see it? I hope so. A land where 'seasons come and go'
Where the 'breezes brush the river on its bars'
Where Aussies living free, only need look up to see
'The wondrous glory of the everlasting stars'.

'In my wild erratic fancy' I reckon that old bushman Clancy
Would be smiling could he see us here today
Then somewhere on the Overflow he would take his hat and throw
It in the air and shout hip hip hooray!

Araluen

To the First Ones.
This is my way of saying sorry in the only way it might do some good.
I hope it empowers you.

Come ye back to Araluen, ancient warrior, distant traveller
Tread ye softly, wake me gently, whisper to me all your woes.
Let the place of waterlilies soothe your pain and ease your sorrow
Sleep forever on my hillside high above the Overflow.

Street of Stones does coldly blackly scatter urchins to and fro
Silence trickles wetly darkly through the lanes of rabbitohs.
Angry alleys shiny prickly wait to hurt the poor of spirit
Dance you through them lonely sadly dreaming of the long ago.

Tears are falling, Moon is weeping, gather up your *pequeninos**
Get thee to a place of shadows, do not listen to the calls.
Whisper there your ancient stories paint your pictures in the caverns
Sing your song so all remember in the time when darkness falls.

All the journeys of a lifetime lead you back to my beginning
To the time before the Dreaming when the Sun beguiled the Moon.
Do you see again your people falling from the stars like raindrops?
Who could hate them, hurt them, steal them, take them from their
        mother's womb?

*A Portuguese word from which, I believe, the English word piccaninny, the offensive
title for an Aboriginal child, is derived.

When the west winds blew the spirits to your homeland's eastern
    doorway
From their cities on the water they seduced you with their songs.
Ran you lightly to the foreshore, waved your arms in laughing welcome
But the spirits took your laughter, put you with the don't belongs.

Many crying, many dying, soon the Dreaming is forgotten
From the tree line you have watched them daring not to get involved.
By 'n' by you come together now you're learning to be stronger
By 'n' by they sign that paper then the problem is resolved.

Come ye back to Araluen, ancient warrior, distant traveller
Tread ye softly, wake me gently, whisper to me all your woes.
Let the place of waterlilies soothe your pain and ease your sorrow
Sleep forever on my hillside high above the Overflow.

The City

Remember Eureka

The H.I.H. collapse 2001

I'm angry, bloody angry and I'm fifty-two years old
Decency's forgotten and the world's gone mad for gold
Where in Christ's name is the honesty that was taught to us as kids
Our country's full of dot com corporate hunters making bids.

Where did we lose our dignity and sense of playing fair
Politicians are in part to blame, but Christ it's ours to share
We voted second-raters to positions of great power
Who let foolish boys with laptops become flavour of the hour.

Now we want to lynch the kids and strip them of their loot
We're saying they are bastards who got too big for their boots
We're screaming that it's their fault paper companies have collapsed
In reality we are having a collective memory lapse.

This is not the first time that the shit has hit the fan
Remember Laurie Connell and Chris Skase the Quintex man
And what of all the 'pyramid' boys and bloody Alan Bond
It was us who let them have their way and even cheered them on.

Well now they're back again these blokes the journos call high-fliers
Because they never had the guts to call them rats and cheats and liars
When Jack Hill the blind miner saw that they weren't worth a zack
Their mates the paper barons warned the journos, 'Watch your backs.'

I think it's time to speak up and ensure some honesty
Is instilled into these bastards who all think they're home scot free
Say, 'By all means do the driving, but don't think you own the car
'And remember that collectively, we're bigger than you are.

'You go ahead and "walk the walk" and play at C.E.O.
'But bear in mind there's all these laid-back fellows called Joe Blow
'And if they get it in their heads your bookwork isn't sound
'You'll go to gaol so bloody fast, your feet won't touch the ground.'

It might frighten the bejesus out of them who's holdin' court
If they realised that some men in this country can't be bought
They'd soon sharpen up their pencils and strengthen their endeavour
If they thought it might be their lips that get sown to-bloody-gether.

I'm not advocating violence but I'm bloody-well pissed off
We've made ourselves a country where we kowtow to the toffs
A simple bloke like me these days is called 'très ordinaire'
By the latte-sipping fat cats who now rape Australia Fair.

It's a lousy situation in this land of milk and honey
When most of us get pissed on by the few who've got the money
The pigs are at the trough again and no one's got the bottle
To rebuild Eureka Stockade and spill blood upon the wattle.

What Do You Want From Me?

I met a bloody wowser who'd been reverent all his life
A pillar of society with a most pretentious wife
They railed upon society, apoplectic in their zest
Making clear to all and sundry they were better than the rest.

He claimed that most within our ranks just do not pull their weight
That some who walk among us are not happy with their fate
Called young ones idle bludgers who will never make the grade
And those who came across the sea all thought they had it made.

He moaned some men are 'different' and their difference is a sin
And 'there should be a barbed-wire cage to lock the buggers in.
'God fearing white Australians should set these matters right!
'And how come hordes of foreigners are claiming civil rights?'

That statement set his missus off and did she go to town
She said, 'Boys should pull up their socks and girls their dresses down
'The streets are full of vagrants and the coppers all are bent.'
And someone had been in their yard and stole her young boy's tent.

So what do you want from me, eh? The answers to it all?
Why some men go on up and up, and some poor bastards fall?
Stop choking me with righteousness, don't quote the sins of man
Just think yourself as lucky that the shit's not hit your fan.

I know a bloke called Terry D, a copper all his life
He works at night in pharmacies to feed his kids and wife
That, rather than go on the take and risk the public ire
Thirty years 'as straight as straight', that's something to admire.

So what do you want from coppers eh? What do you want to see?
A world that's safe to walk in and free from anarchy?
Take a look around you, mate, and tell me what you spot?
It's not so bad, you must admit, there's 'haves' and there's 'have nots'.

I know a bloke called Benny E, a vagrant who's all right
He has to steal in winter time to get a bed at night
But better gaol than in the park and freezing bloody cold
Even city vagrants want to live until they're old.

So what do you want from vagrants, eh? Don't want them to steal?
The world can be a lonely place when you can't get a meal
Take a look around you two and tell me what's the form?
Would you risk the park each night? At least a prison's warm.

I know a bloke called Alfie G, a 'tea leaf' all his life
He works each night at larceny, but has no gun or knife
A 'straight-up' crook who knows the game and always 'cops it sweet'
A nicer, softer, petty thief you'd never chance to meet.

So what do you want from 'tea leaves', eh? They're harmless parasites
They spend their days seeking ways to crack a job at night
So one of them just pinched your tent, you don't put on a blue
You walk a mile in Alfie's shoes then tell me what you'd do?

Terry, Ben and Alfie meet each year on Anzac Day
Their lifestyles are forgotten as they kneel at dawn and pray
As they get drunk by 'shout' in turn and relive their lost dreams
The things you two go on about seem cheap in the extreme.

I know so many people just like Terry, Alf and Ben
And I know Arabs, Jews and Abos and the girl in number ten
She's a hooker and she's honest and can be a bloody hoot
And I'll tell you both for nothing, we both smoke a bit of 'toot'!

So what do I want from you? you ask. You're wowsers, so it seems
Stop whingeing for a minute, know that everyone has dreams
Those men I've mentioned do it hard, poor Benny's life's a sewer
But I'd bet my bottom dollar they're all better men than you are.

Jeez S.T.

Can you understand the GST? I know I bloody can't
Neither can my cousin or my sister or my aunt
I'm not Albert Einstein, but then I'm nobody's fool
I done arithmetic and writing and I learned the golden rule.

I'm just your ordinary bloke and I've gone all right till now
I've always done my income tax though it's a bloody cow
This GST has got me stuffed, it's harder than before
What I always did just once a year I now do bloody four.

Everyone had two bob's worth while makin' the new law
The only ones who had no say were the elderly or poor
The Libs and Labs and Democrats got at each other's throats
And made it such a bun fight no one quite knew how to vote.

The unions spat the dummy while the rich just didn't care
The farmers did their lolly, said the fuel tax wasn't fair
The public service sniggered and the Greens let out a holler
Why couldn't they have all agreed on ten cents in the dollar?

The ATO's no place to go and ask a civil question
The only thing you'll get from them is indi-bloody-gestion
I asked them 'What's the difference 'tween a chicken and a 'roo?'
They said I was a smartarse and we all got in a blue.

Now the ATO have told me that if chook is raw or cooked
I have to work out what I pay or I'll get bloody booked!
Do I really care? It's just not fair! I'm going off my head!
And the chicken don't care either 'cause the chicken's bloody dead!

Children of God

Fair play, I say to the boy in the gutter
He made it this far on his own
Mind you he's only eleven years old
And he knew that his chances were blown.

But an ambo pulls an adrenalin stick
And drives it straight into his chest
Kick-starts his heart and brings the lad back
To suffer again with the rest.

Up in Kings Cross in a world of their own
They fight and they lie and they steal
And anything else they're required to do
If it brings them the money to deal.

They are children of God brought to their knees
Through no real fault of their own
Abused by their parents or used by their friends
They've wandered away all alone.

And the streets hold no pity in this bloody city
Especially for unwanted kids
No place to live and a cold night or two
And most of them take to the skids.

They start out just hanging like others
With similar stories and living on hope
But life soon divides them and cold abuse guides them
Straight to the end of a rope.

But don't you feel bad, put your hand in your bag
When the Salvos hit your door
Give up five bucks for the kids on the streets
And another five bucks for the poor.

Hold the euphoria, taste the elation
Feel your pulse race to the max
Your conscience is clear for another full year
And you'll get the ten back in your tax.

Meanwhile in the Cross with the rest of the dross
Another young boy hits the smack
A twelve-year-old girl earns the money to join him
By just lying down on her back.

She doesn't know but the boy's overdosed
For the score he injected was shit
The bloke grunting over the twelve-year-old girl
Doesn't care, he's just after a bit.

Her memory fades as the bloke contracts AIDS
And it serves the bastard right
He'll head for his comfortable house in the suburbs
And sleep with his wife tonight.

And when they find out that they're going to die
They'll cry and ask the priest why?
But he'll have no answer, he'll just shake his head
And dumbly point at the sky.

The girl dreams of home, not the one she is from
But one full of love and affection
She asks of the man, 'Will you be my daddy?'
As he angrily thrusts his erection.

'Please take me home with you, mister?' she asks.
'You can do it to me every day.'
He guiltily dresses and goes on his way
Unaware that the piper's been paid.

Back in the alley she bites on the rubber
To tighten her tourniquet
She lies by the boy now knowing he's dead
And syringes herself away.

Off to the land of dreams she rushes
She sighs and begins to nod
A cop finds them dead the very next morning
And weeps for the children of God.

Forever then . . .

I watched a small boy at the edge of the sea, building a castle of sand
He swore an oath to defend the right and excitedly raised his hand
With a stick for a sword, against a horde of crabs he defended the moat
And I wanted so much to be part of it all the breath caught in my throat.

A dragon attacked him from out of the sun and forced him into the waves
'A curse on you beast,' he valiantly cried. 'Now see how a knight behaves.'
He parried and thrust with his trusty blade and struck a mortal blow
Then muttered a spell in an ancient tongue that only a boy can know.

A surfboat raced down the front of a wave and carved its way to shore
'Vikings, sir knight!' I wanted to call, 'There must be fifty or more!'
'I'd given ye up for dead, me lads,' he yelled, as the bow hit sand
'Haul her up on the beach, me boys, we've a dangerous job to hand.'

As the boat crew hauled their craft above the tide marks on the beach
'I've done for the pirates alone,' he cried. 'The treasure's within our reach!'
They all ignored the boy on the beach; they were adults after all
But he babbled on happily sharing his dream 'til he heard his mother call.

'Away from them son, they've work to do. Their job is saving life.'
That stopped the lad, momentarily, but he soon invented more strife
'Who be ye?' he asked at once of his feisty cattle dog pup
'Be ye a spotted blue hound from hell the Devil has sent me up?'

Blue could tell by his master's voice it was time to make an escape
But before he could bolt the hell hound killer had scruffed him by the nape
'Not so fast, my spotted friend, you'll answer and pay for your crimes!'
He wrapped a towel round Bluey's neck and tugged it several times.

'Don't hurt the dog,' his mother crooned as only a mother can
So the boy released his faithful mate, who fell on his head in the sand
'Why is the sky that blue, Mum,' he asked, 'a different blue to the sea?'
'Why don't you ask your father,' she said, then looked directly at me.

'Dad wouldn't know how to answer that, Mum, he's just not one for talk.'
I could only sit and stare at my son as he took the pup for a walk
'It's bad enough that he only sees you every second week.
  'The least you could do for the poor little bugger is let him hear
      you speak.'

'How could you do it to me and the boy? Leave us alone like you've done?
'I'm finding it so bloody hard at the moment. Not what you'd call a
      good run.
'I suppose you've a girlfriend these days, with your charm? Hope it's no
      one that I know.'
'Give it a rest. Here's the money.' I said. 'I'm sorry, I have to go.'

'It must be so lovely to get up and go and not feel responsible!
'How can you have a small boy and not love him? It should
      be impossible!'
I let all the pain in her voice hit my back as I walked to the top of
      the beach
And made it back to the street where I hoped the bitterness
      wouldn't reach.

I watched a small boy at the edge of the sea, building a castle of sand
He swore an oath to defend the right and excitedly raised his hand
With a stick for a sword, against a horde of crabs he defended the moat
And I wanted so much to be part of it all the breath caught in my throat.

The Kids in the Sea

The boy stood on the burning deck and jumped into the sea
Or so the bloody P.M. said, what sort of bloke is he?

Phil Ruddock said it too, you know, and so did Peter Reith
As they watched the cauldron bubble like the witches on the heath.

The Admiral he drank from it and so did Robert Hill
And Oakes asked of the Admiral, 'Do you feel like a dill?'

When Chris called short his conference McPhedran flew him too
Like all the other pressmen in the gallery he knew.

That there was something rotten in the state of A.C.T.
And one more question might reveal a 'Kids Conspiracy'.

Bill Leak tore bloody strips off them as only Leak can do
And Warren from the *Telegraph*, he tore a few off too.

Did thoughts of mothers throwing little kids into the ocean
Get them re-elected on a groundswell of emotion?

Did they let a lie remain to get their bloody way
On November bloody ten, the day before Remembrance Day?

Lest we forget! They would have murmured on that holiest of mornings
Lest we forget what? is now the question that is dawning.

Do we forgo the truth now and risk our democracy?
We must demand the truth about those 'kids thrown in the sea'.

An Opening at Last

What did you say to your mates, Ocker
After you'd watched the show?
Did you get stuck into it all, mate
Or give it a fair dinkum go?

I know you well by now, Ocker
Just let me guess what you said
'The opening was a disaster,' right?
'The committee is stuffed in the head'?

I can hear you now at the bar, Ocker
'It was all so much bullshit,' right?
Running your country into the ground
Until you started a fight.

Why don't you give it a rest, Ocker?
Australia's left you behind
The people were proud of that ceremony
Can't you take that as a sign?

The Kooris showed such dignity, Ocker
They made me feel so proud
Their songs of the Dreamtime got me in
Along with the rest of the crowd.

And what of the singers and dancers, Ocker?
People of every creed
Joined together as Aussies, mate
Fused by a single need.

They made the show a beauty, Ocker
And stuck it right up you
You're a bloody dinosaur, mate
And so is your point of view.

Sydney
19 October 2000

Olympicked Out

Sixteen bloody days of it and I've got bloody piles
From sitting on my bum at the TV
My wife's gone to her sister's and the dog has starved to death
They're prob'ly both far better off than me.

I've been eating bloody baked beans till they're coming out my ears
And drinking like a bloody man possessed
I've been screaming with emotion at the bloody Aussie team
Until I realised I was bloody well obsessed.

I started emulating all the things our athletes did
By leaping chairs and chucking pots and pans
I got so bloody heated when the hammer throw came on
I tossed the cat into the ceiling fan.

Clunk he went, then he took off for all that he was worth
Luckily I knew where he would go
And I caught the little bastard at the top of the side gate
'Cause the Aussie bloke still had another throw.

And when the Aussie sheila in the water polo team
Threw the winning goal you would have laughed
I stripped down to my undies, threw the cat into the shower
And dived head first into the bloody bath.

I shot the neighbour's cocky when Mike Diamond shot for gold
And used my shotgun as a bloody bat
When that gorgeous Aussie shortstop hit a home run to left field
I hit the cat for one! How good was that!

And here comes Cathy Freeman! That's what I was bloody screamin'
As she came out of the turn into the straight
And when she hit the line I yelled, 'You bloody little beauty!'
And asked the cat, 'Just how good is she, mate?'

He was perched up on the bookshelf, thinking he was safe
Staring down like only cats can do
But when that 'drop dead' Aussie Tatiana won the silver
I grabbed the broom and vaulted up there too.

He sensed I was deranged so he took off for the toilet
But I'd just seen the Aussie fellas dive
I did a double somersault with pike and half a twist
That dive was worth at least a nine point five.

But I forgot about the cat when I looked up at the telly
There were Roy and H.G. on the late late show
They had a fat-arsed wombat with a knife stuck in its bum
And they'd named the funny little fellow Fatso.

The little wombat's arse was as big as West Australia
And his eyes said he'd been recently desexed
The cat looked at the wombat then he caught my glazed expression
And took off thinking maybe he was next.

But my bloody glazed expression was due to what came on the telly
What a way to end the bloody night!
Kevan Gosper, Mister Coates and those other SOCOG bastards
Posing with that wowser Michael Knight.

With that image it all ended, the whole Olympic Games
For a moment I was utterly despondent
But! If I sue for divorce (I'll ask to keep the cat, of course)
I'll name those bloody bastards co-respondents.

After that, four years of peace unless of course the bloody Greeks
Fail to live up to their bloody expectations
They'd better pull their fingers out because I'm Olympicked out
And there's enough heroes already in this nation.

By Christ I hope they do, because I'm bloody telling you
Sixteen days of competition's done my kidneys
The stakes are just too high. Me and the cat'd prob'ly die
If they brought the bloody games back here to Sydney.

My Camera My Arse!

The night too quickly passes now here in this sunburnt land
But that's all right, the cricket ground's got lights above the stand
Don't wait for Sat'dy arvo like they did in the old days
Now they've got sport on every night, of course it's user pays.

You don't watch the vision splendid from the sunlit plains extended
You watch the Sumo wrestlers goin' at it, gut extended
TV's the go, it's got it all, from Fight Night to the ponies
You watch them in your lounge room and get pissed with all
        your cronies.

There's no biffo in the scrum these days, that's all in the past
'Cause now they've got a 'bum-cam' stuck right up the hooker's arse
And when you watch the motorcycle champion flying past
There's one hooked up in his bum too, to see who's coming last!

Clancy's gone up Queensland drovin', but we don't care where 'e are
There's motor heads on Panorama screaming in their cars
And when some yob oils up the road to make a driver skid
What's there? A bloody 'crash-cam' mate, to film the one who did.

That peaceful silence of the mind when on a cattle drive
Can't compare to watching all those Yank rodeos 'live'
And when a cowboy hits the turf, hey, what's that in his arse?
A bloody 'bull-cam' you can bet! Those Yank shows are all class.

And what about the League boys on the telly with their show
Every night a different frock, their hair done up in bows
Mind you it makes you wonder, they're all ex-Kangaroos
Just what went on, on British tours, and what was stuck up who?

And what about the newest show from China called *Inject*?
They stick a 'blood-cam' in the arm of any they suspect
The tiny little camera goes a-sneaking through their veins
If anyone is caught out they're required to name names.

It was used in the Olympics and by Christ it caused a buzz
There was so much bloody name droppin' they had to call the Fuzz
And those who did get lumbered, specially if they were 'Austrayun'
Had to melt their medals down for fines that needed payin'.

I didn't care! From my armchair I just screamed, 'Gold! Gold! Gold!'
That's right! From my armchair, mate! All the tickets had been sold.
They went to SOCOG members and their kids and VIPs!
You didn't really think they'd come to folks like you and me?

We're the great unwashed, mate! Get your sports priorities right!
We're not like politicians who get in for free each night
We're ordinary, you and me. That's why there's '*pay*' TV
So we can stay at home you dill! And watch it free, you see!

Yeah give me TV any day. My digital, my call!
I'm all prepared. Got booze and food. I'm gonna watch it all
I've only got one small concern, this 'view-cam', that's not on!
They stick it up the viewer's arse, but they don't turn it on!

Centre Stage

I have great respect and affection for actors, and theatre actors particularly. Although some are self-obsessed to the point of distraction, they are in the main honest, intelligent, dedicated people. They devote their lives to a difficult and unforgiving profession for ultimately very little reward, except perhaps for the intermittent, euphoric glow that descends upon them with the curtain. I have felt that glow several times and understand the desire for it. It is unquenchable.

The Mermaid Tavern, Swan and Globe
Were of the golden age
When wond'rous words were boldly writ
And roared from centre stage.

Know you this place, this centre stage?
The loneliest on earth
Where only strong of heart would tread
To play with grief and mirth.

The Bard, the Spy, the Burbage men
Took centre stage in turn
They strode the boards and took their stance
Out where the pin spot burns.

It's not for faint of heart, the stage
You're seen for what you are
But men and women strong of heart
Can shine there like the stars.

They make you laugh, they make you cry
As they perform each eve
They share with you their muse of fire
You'll beg them not to leave.

Yet leave they will eventually
All curtains must come down
Then, if you dare to follow them
Their smiles will turn to frowns.

Unless of course you smile and nod
Discreetly, it must seem
They'll glow demurely for they'll know
You've recognised their dream.

The world in which actors exist
It turns from page to page
It spins from act to act each night
Its axis, centre stage.

They live in a kaleidoscope
And share a thousand lives
Whirling in their written world
Until *finis* arrives.

So, judge them not in their domain
But walk you soft away
For as in life remember, with
No cast there is no play.

Hey Diddle Dee Dee

Dedicated to the staff of NIDA and its graduates. Inspired after a chat at the NIDA bar with John Clark and others, at the conclusion of a third-year graduation performance. Our discourse on the vagaries of acting, humorously sprinkled with the high camp vocabulary unique to that profession, revealed to me a genuinely fine man with a great love for the institution he serves and the actors it creates.

What is there, twixt life and death? The play that comes between
It's called an actor's life my friend and you're in every scene.

You've got the lead! You're dressed for it! You're even of the age!
Oh, by the way darl', that's your mark, the chalk at centre stage.

Now, hold the thought that you're the best the Roscius of your age
And don't trip over the furniture when you get out on stage.

Then take your stance and give your best, and make sure you project
And don't forget who's 'out in front', your every move is checked.

The 'bums on seats' have paid the price to laugh at you, or cry
So give them all their money's worth and make sure you don't dry.

And some will want a tragedy and some will want a laugh
It matters not! The main thing is you're not late for 'the half'.

Now, half an hour is half an hour to anyone alive
But when you work in theatre, pet, 'the half' is thirty-five.

Remember it's a theatre, dear, and not a crematorium
Be sure to use the stage door, sweetie, not the auditorium.

For God's sake please don't whistle! Never quote the Scottish play!
And tell your rellies 'don't send lilies' on your day of days.

And don't defer daylight employ, except for matinees
Be aware that you must eat and there's the rent to pay.

So 'chookers' to you, thespian! Go strut your worldly stage!
I'll pray you reach that final play, the one they call 'Old Age'.

And bear in mind, through all of it, the most important factor
You're the one who blithely said, 'I want to be an actor.'

War and Remembrance

Remembrance Day

On the eleventh of November in the year nineteen eighteen
At eleven of the clock a silence fell
Shell-shocked men stood staring blankly, thinking, finally it's over
Then a distant steeple chimed a mournful bell.

All at once a hundred lifetimes passed before a million eyes
As mates remembered mates from long ago
Then they crossed the dreaded No Man's Land, now just a piece of earth
And bade farewell to those who'd been their foe.

Had it been a hundred lifetimes or just four short bloody years
Since they'd left 'down under' for those foreign shores?
Was it all an awful dream or had those dreadful battles happened
And if they'd happened what had been the cause?

'Didn't some Serb shoot an Archduke?' said a vacant-eyed young Aussie
'Wasn't that what started all the fuss?'
'That's about the strength of it,' a Kiwi sergeant muttered
'Though Christ knows what it had to do with us.'

'Sabre rattling,' said another, 'by antiquated royal families
And their stupid bloody-minded politicians
Screaming "fight for King and Country" and "defend our sovereign honour"
While they used us all as human ammunition.'

'I'm just glad the killing's over,' sighed a sad boy of eighteen
'I'm going home to have the best time ever.'
An older soldier's glance revealed to all that young boy's chance
Of recapturing his youth had gone forever.

They'd grown old within a nightmare from which they would never wake
It would stay with them through all their coming years
They'd be ancients walking backwards to the light of childhood dreams
Glowing faintly through a misty veil of tears.

Then as one they turned and shuffled through the trenches to the rear
As they walked the memories came flooding back
Of the good times back in Cairo when the friendships had begun
And much further back along the wallaby track.

But then came the names and visions of strange places they had been
And the faces of the mates who'd fought and fell
Shrapnel Gully, Lone Pine Ridge and the Nek and Chunuk Bair
Where the Kiwis briefly glimpsed the Dardenelles.

In the Holy Land, Beersheba, where the Light Horse charged the wells
And the aftermath of that valiant attack
When they had to shoot their horses so they wouldn't be abused
'Cause the bloody army wouldn't ship them back.

Then the fiery hell of Flanders and Saint Quentin and Verdun
And the reckless valour shown at Passchendaele.
Through the madness of the Somme when their world was an inferno
Never once did Anzac courage ever fail.

One by one they turned in rifles, bandoliers and pannikins
Then a man began to hum an Aussie song
And they sang 'Waltzing Matilda' as they marched towards the south
Back down under to the countries they belonged.

Each November the eleventh at eleven in the morning
Imagine will you please, a gold sunset?
Bow your head for just a minute and I swear you'll hear a bugle
Call for all of those who fell. Lest We Forget.

Mates

Jesus! Jimmy tell them I died bravely for my country
Don't tell them I was clinging to the earth
Tell them I put up a fight and that I was doing right
Say I got stuck in for all that I was worth.

You did, mate. So did Kenny and the old man and the boys
The whole damn lot of you did bloody fine
Stop talking now and listen there's a doctor down the line
You'll be right again, just give it time.

What they're asking us to do is flaming mad I'm telling you
We'll get our own C.O. before too long
Maybe General Monash, he's a good bloke so I've heard
And soon we'll be back home where we belong.

We're Anzacs, mate! We'll do this mob in no time! Mark my words!
In the meantime you lie back and try to rest
Oh crikey, mate! The bloody bleeding's starting up again
I can't stop it, Alf, I'm giving it my best.

Alfie, please don't leave me. Come on, mate, you're doing fine!
Christ! We're stuck out here beyond the wire
Oh no! Here they come again and there's hundreds more of them
We're for it, mate, they're going to open fire!

Am I lying in the dirt? God, when those bullets hit they hurt
But the pain's gone and that says I'm going to die
I'm coming with you, mate, and I reckon that's just great
It means that we don't have to say goodbye.

The Simpson Prize Winners

Inspired by a story of two young Simpson Prize winners, Nikki Macor and
Lachlan Foy, who visited Lone Pine, Gallipoli, in 1999

Near a beach in far off Turkey on the twenty-fifth of April
Stood an Aussie girl and boy of tender years
They had come to offer thanks to all the Anzacs who had fallen
On the hills of death that hold our nation's tears.

They were staring at the gravestone of one John Simpson Kirkpatrick
Who, with his donkey 'Murphy', won such fame
Taking wounded to the beaches through the hell of Shrapnel Gully
Until the bullet came that held his name.

The grave alongside Simpson's sadly bore no epitaph
A voice said, 'No one loved him,' with a sigh
Among the ghosts of fallen Anzacs that young girl then softly whispered
'I love him,' and the boy said, 'So do I.'

The Last Sunset

Aired nationally on radio, Remembrance Day 2000

In a foreign field a young soldier lay dying in the rain
When to his dreams there came a girl he knew
She kissed his lips and then she placed a poppy in his hand
And suddenly the sky turned azure blue.

He heard a morning magpie and a kookaburra laugh
A brumby whinny and a stockwhip crack
He heard the distant sound of wild thunder in the ranges
And a Melbourne tram go rattling down the track.

He saw the far Blue Mountains and the surf at Bondi Beach
He watched the sun rise over Morton Bay
He was smiling as the sun set slowly on the River Somme
And with the death of day he passed away.

On the eleventh of November you make sure that you remember
That boy who clutched the poppy to his breast
Say thank you for his courage, whisper soft 'lest we forget'
And with all your heart wish him eternal rest.

Sport

Southern Brothers

Way down in the Southern Ocean in the reckless latitudes
Where the roarin' forties make the careless pay
Lie three nations proud and mighty with defiant attitudes
Who aren't afraid to stand and have their say.

Each year the three do battle for a prize worth more than gold
 In stadiums throughout their noble lands
Like knights of old they fight, and the oath, 'Defend the Right!'
Is demanded by the crowds who pack the stands.

The prize is like the World Cup in the Southern Hemisphere
To win it is each nation's highest aim
For to raise that trophy skywards in those wild lands down under
Means you are the greatest at the game.

They are hard men who contest it, men from harsh environments
Men of iron will in fearful combinations
They fight for sporting glory at the game of rugby union
In the series known to all as the Tri-Nations.

One hundred and ten thousand will, in Stadium Australia
Roar their hearts out for the Wallabies
And Ballymore goes crazy when they see their favourite sons
In green and gold take on their enemies.

In New Zealand at Dunedin there's a place called House of Pain
And Eden Park's a house of derring-do
They are All Black battlegrounds where no quarter's ever given
And Maori gods protect the chosen few.

'Nkosi sikelel' iAfrika!' roar the men who wear the Springbok
When any team dares enter Ellis Park
And Nedlands is a place to chill the bravest of men's souls
Where only heroes ever leave their mark.

But at all those famous grounds no matter which team's going round
Men shake hands in open admiration
For on the turf and in the stands, mate, the folk of three great lands
Make friendships that will last for generations.

Southern nations! Southern brothers! All Blacks! Springboks! Wallabies!
Hear our voices from the bottom of the world
Place your hand over your heart when you hear the anthems start
And sing out as you watch the flags unfurl.

The greatest bonds of friendship are those ones forged in battle
So play it hard no matter what the cost
But when the battle's done, shake the hands of those who won
And shake too, the hands of those who lost.

To do so gives you honour and respect among your peers
A handshake costs you nothing but your time
Friendship is the only motive to ever play a game
All else is left to reason and to rhyme.

On starry southern nights, crowds will roar 'Defend the Right!'
And feel the sudden rush of jubilation
As they sit and watch the best, in rugby union's hardest tests
The series known to all as the Tri-Nations.

Sydney
29 July 2000

The Yaapie, the Kiwi and Me

Addendum to Southern Brothers
(Based on a true story)

Way down in the Southern Ocean in the reckless latitudes
Where the roarin forties make the careless pay
Live three men proud and mighty with defiant attitudes
Who aren't afraid to stand and have their say.

Men of stature, men of breeding, men of massive intellect
Men who've supped beneath the ancient Knowledge Tree
One's a Yaapie, very simple, one's a Kiwi, also simple
And the third in the triumvirate is me.

And so it came to pass that I was sitting on my arse
With these two friends I've known for many years
Kenny Smith from Timaru, a rabid All Black through and through
And a 'Bok from Stellenbosch called Jan De Beers.

We'd had a lot of drink and I was feeling in the pink
Chauvinistic and I mean that literally
No prefix 'male' and suffix 'pig', I really wanted them to dig
The fact that I'm a lover of my country.

In green and gold regalia I stood in Stadium Australia
Waxing lyrical about the place
Till the Yaapie and the Kiwi, unannounced went for a wee-wee
And left me chatting to an empty space.

When they came back they were blueing, rather heatedly arguing
About the merits of our three great nations
Kenny said that he was proud of the Land of Long White Cloud
But Jannie had a different explanation.

'The people of New Zealand love to be all warm and friendly
'And offer you the chance to enter Eden
'Then they unleash the bloody All Blacks on you like a pack of ridgebacks
'Who chase you all the way down to Dunedin.

'And once there they smile again. "Welcome to the House of Pain"
'They say, grinning as you stare over your shoulder
'And there's the All Blacks once again, who chase you through the
        freezing rain
'To Invercargill where it's even bloody colder.

'Listen to me now, meineer, the bloody Kiwis are all queer
'And I'm not putting in the boot now
'Only they would build a town, paint all the buildings mission brown
'And call the bloody place Waikikamukau.

'I ask you! Can you tell me what other race of people
'Ties a piece of rope around their "ligs"
'Then like a shot out of a gun – and they call this having fun –
'Jump head first off a bloody bridge?'

That's when Kenny spat the dummy, stared through eyes a little rummy
And sneered, 'You lussen here Jannie De Beer
'You take beck all you sid or I'll het you on the hid
'How deer you say New Zellenders are queer.'

71

'Ach, Kenny, Kenny, Kenny,' Jannie said. 'There aren't that many
'Kiwis that I really can't abide
'Just those from North and South, then there's you and your big mouth
'And the whole New Zealand rugby union side.'

'Right, right, right!' Kenny yelled. 'We're gonna fight!
'I'll warn you now before I bleddy hut you
'I was taught to use karate by my old Chinese aunty
'End I've got a bleck belt un Jepenase ju jutsu.'

'Jannie, Jannie, Jannie,' I said. 'I find it kind of funny
'When you say there's not a Kiwi of whom you're fond
'Surely somewhere in the past you must have kissed somebody's arse
'Who hailed from the far side of the pond?'

Then it was Kenny's turn to speak. Usually he's rather meek
But this time we'd both gone a bit too far
'If all you do es teek the puss, I thenk I'll gev the geem a muss!'
Then he stood up and walked off to the bar.

'Now see there, you've upset him!' Jannie said. 'How can you let him
'Go wandering off to get drunk all alone?'
'I've upset him? Damn it, Jannie, you're the one who got him barmy
'Telling him that sheep could now be cloned!'

Ken came back a while later and said, 'I'm un a bitter state
'Of mind thin I was un a while before
'Ut's jist thet I git so vucious lustening to all the pernucious
'Ravings of thet awful luttle Boer.'

As I moved off to buy a round I saw a team run on the ground
And sensed the Yaapie and the Kiwi freeze
'They're the Swans!' Jannie hissed. 'Ach, man! I can't believe this!
'Where are the bloody 'Boks and Wallabies?'

You wouldn't want to bloody know, all day I'd had the pair in tow
And between each pub I'd shown them Sydney Town
But we got pissed as rabbits, and then by force of habit
I took them to the Sydney Cricket Ground.

On the train at Central Station after missing the Tri-Nations
We agreed the night had been rather absurd
And travelled home in silence entertaining thoughts of violence
Towards each other – but no one said a word.

Way down in the Southern Ocean where the greatest rugby's played
Three mates set off to go to Homebush Bay
But they got drunk, you see . . . and wound up in the S.C.G.
It's a secret they've kept to this very day.

Sydney
29 July 2000

Ode to Norm

Heroes on telly every night!
The fastest, the fittest the best!
Football and racing, rugby and fights
Cricket one-dayers and Tests.

During the day you keep watching away
With the best in the world on your set
You'll see the gee-gees from here to the bush
Get on the phone! Have a bet!

I saw a kid on a snowboard last night
Fly through the air like a bird
No! I'm not kidding. He was terrific
For once I was lost for words.

Flying through space down a mountainside
Just like a bat out of Hell
While I just sat staring, mesmerised
Caught up in a magical spell.

I'm telling you, mate, he'd leave us for dead
In the old days down Billycart Hill
If you and me tried to do what he did
I reckon we'd 'av'ta take pills.

The sports they play now are out of our league
Some is real dangerous stuff
You wouldn't catch me doing those sorts of things
They're made of much sterner stuff.

A bloke on the telly was saying next week
They've got some fella, it seems
Climbing an ice face in Switzerland
It's a sport that he calls 'extreme'.

You gotta hand it to those cameramen
Sport's a new world for me
The sort of shows they put on now
Are really something to see.

Parachuting! Rifle shooting!
Surfing, that's the go!
Not like you and me, old mate
All those years ago.

Kids put sails on surfboards now
And spin up through the air
Somersaults they do these days!
And we thought we were lairs.

They fly in planes, fight bulls in Spain
And climb the craziest places
But what I like the most of all's
The looks upon the faces.

We're past it now, mate, you and I
That's the honest truth
Would you trade everything you own
For one more taste of youth?

To feel the sun upon your face
The wind against your skin
Can you remember, china plate
What it felt like to win?

To kick a goal or toss a pole
To run and jump and leap?
That fire's there in memory still
For me each night in sleep.

But I can feel the next best thing
To fire in the belly
Any time I want 'cause I
Can watch it on the telly.

You think I'm joking? Watch tonight
'Cause what I'm saying's true
Telly makes the memories
Come flooding back to you.

Ready . . . Set . . . No!

I must confess to being a couch potato when it comes to sport. I'm as guilty as Norm when it comes to one-day cricket or any of the football codes, and I admire any champion for the perseverance and dedication they display in achieving Olympic and international success. However, I feel duty bound to say something about the adulation afforded such people, by Australians in particular. The village idiot can run 100 metres—I know this to be true because I have done it. And I can even swim that distance. I can also jump, throw, kick, hit and catch. While I don't do any of them very well, I can do them, that is, until dotage and senility catch up with me. Therefore, I personally place little importance on these abilities. Ergo, I further reason, the only differences between myself and an Olympic gold medallist are age, ability and a desire to win that, quite frankly, never occurred to me.

The ability to achieve sporting immortality does not require a degree in quantum physics. Australians with great minds who achieve international recognition in their chosen fields of endeavour are rarely esteemed or admired as much as our sports champions. This situation must be redressed, or the cost of living room furniture and root vegetables is going to skyrocket!

He runs, she swims, he jumps, she squats
He leaps, she hits, he bats, so what?

They mix, they eight, they four, they pair
They play, they win, but I don't care.

There's more to life than bat and glove
There's war, and peace, and hate, and love.

The games of life and death, that we
Must win, to serve humanity.

We need the sword to fight the foe
But we need more than that, you know.

It takes a mind, to fight a war
The pen will beat the sword, for sure.

Pure physical ability
Has never won a war, you see

So run and jump both broad and long
Ensure our citizens are strong.

But don't forget, it's brains we need
In life, if we are to succeed.

The Girl on the Bridge

Nakao Takahashi

I saw a girl on a bridge today
She smiled and waved at me.
Running towards the west she was
To a date with destiny.

She'd win the Olympic marathon
And make her day of days
But she did something more for me
On that bridge in a different way.

To the west there stands a soldier
He rests on arms reversed
And when she ran beneath the span
At first it seemed perverse.

Then I suddenly thought the tune she hears
Has a modern melody
She runs to the beat of a different drum
Because she is young and free.

There and then my soul took flight
Weight lifted from my heart
That girl and I were suddenly close
Where we'd been worlds apart.

She'll never know what she achieved
As she traversed that span
The bridge she crossed was the Anzac Bridge
And the girl was from Japan.

Give Me the Rush

You know how it feels like there's wings on your heels
There are butterflies deep in your gut
The bowler runs in and the air's full of swing
And you know that it's there to be cut.

The batsman leans back and then there's a crack
And the whole stadium goes berserk
You roar till you cry, then bite into your pie
And keep watching that Aussie boy work.

It's the same at the 'G' when the Blues get a free
And the forward is sixty m out
You watch the kick fly until you see sky
And the umpire sticks both fingers out.

Or you're out at the track and you hear the crack
Of the whips as the horses roar past
You cheer as the champ, on the race sets his stamp
And your pals yell out, 'Mate, is he fast?'

Forward on forward, lock against lock
The ball fires out to the wing
Through the centres it passes, you watch through your glasses
That feeling can make your heart sing.

Mate, it's a rush! It makes the blood flush
Through your system, it pounds in your ears
The winger goes over, the game is all over!
And you sit back and drink in the cheers.

I've seen them all mate, games from every state
And others from all round the earth
Any sport you can name, I'm into the game
And I barrack for all that I'm worth.

The Proteas, Pakis, Windies or Poms
I'm telling you I've got the urge
One-dayers and Tests, I must see the best!
I love that adrenalin surge.

Show me the Fox! Stream the game to the box!
I want adrenalin plus!
Man U, Swans, Razors, the Roosters, the Sox!
Go for it! Give me the rush!

The Catch

As far as I remember it was early in December
I was fielding in the slips next door to Ponting
The pommie batsman edged a ball, not a real good shot at all
When I quickly realised that I was wanting.

Waugh and Gilchrist yelled out 'Catch it!' But I knew I couldn't match it
It was coming at me like a Kenworth truck
Hayden yelled out 'Mate, it's yours!' As I went down on all fours
'Cause I'd made my mind up I was gonna duck.

It hit one of my joints then it flew straight out to point
Where Justin Langer lost his timing
Then it shot towards the stumps where it nearly hit the ump
It hit Gillespie then shot out to Symonds.

He was in the deepest cover and was fighting off a plover
Who was trying vainly to protect its nest
It hit the bird and killed it, then something supernatural willed it
Out to fine leg where young Lee gave it his best.

Brett flipped it up to Martyn and it set his fingers smartin'
But he knocked it up for Glen McGrath, you see
Glen went flat out to get to it and he just managed to screw it
Off his knee cap and the ball came back to me.

It just popped into my hands and the fans up in the stands
Let out a roar that Bradman couldn't match
Then the greatest thing of all, Stevie Waugh looked at the ball
Then shook his head and said, 'Mate, what a catch!'

As tears of joy bedimmed my eyes I turned to both umpires
And slowly I took off my baggy hat
I raised the ball up to the sky and with an air of princely pride
I yelled at both those umpires, 'How was that?'

Then I heard my missus screaming, 'How was what? You're
      bloody dreaming!
'Get out of bed, you useless drip!'
I just leant back on my pillow and saw again the flash of willow
As I caught that pommie batsman in the slips.

Hong Kong

Fragrant Harbour

Heung Gong

I see a fragrant harbour lit up by a China moon
The smell of jasmine haunts my midnight mind
I hear the sound of wind chimes and the sad cry of the loon
As my memory goes marching back through time.

When I call back all those yesterdays I see two almond eyes
Blazing with an oriental fire
A green and golden *cheung sam* that is split from knee to thigh
Stirs again the embers of desire.

I was one of many misfits in a far off foreign land
Wanderlust had cast me on its shore
And I marched with Chinese pipers and a military band
And saw things I had never seen before.

Like snakes curled up in crystal jars and lanterns on the sea
Lions in the streets and *dai pai dongs**
Where I drank the *Tsing Tao* amber and ate the sweet *lai chi*
And sang the melancholy Gaelic songs.

I still see the smiling faces of the people in the streets
And the ferries with the ensign of the star
And smell again the *char siu*** and the oriental sweets
And the raucous '*Jo san Dai Loh, nei ho ma?*'

* *Street food stall – 'dai pai' means big paper and refers to the licence required to operate the stall.*
** *Barbecued pork.*

'Good morning, Elder Brother, are you well or are you not?'
The singsong question always made me smile
'Sit and sip some jasmine, can you sit or can you not?'
They'd call out over rattling *mah-jong* tiles.

Oh so many sights and sounds now join the bright procession
That meanders like a river through my brain
Fleeting glimpses, first impressions, noisy Chinese opera sessions
And the rat-tat-tat of Oriental rain.

Dancing dragons, fire crackers, cymbals, drums and village bands
The gentle tinkle of the temple bells
Tug boats, junks, black contraband, cargo ships from foreign lands
And silent gunboats riding ocean swells.

I hear still the stamp of boot studs and the beating of my heart
In that silence after rifle bolts are locked
When the world stops for a second just before the troubles start
Then the chaos, as the universe is rocked.

Of all memories I have, though, one's far stronger than the others
And it comes upon me when I hear the songs
That I sang with all those misfits I remember as my brothers
We were policemen in a city called Hong Kong.

Hong Kong Song

From the Peak, 1977

There's a city up in Asia
Nestled in the China Sea
It's the mother of all misfits
And a port for refugees
It is known as 'Fragrant Harbour'
Though it contradicts the name
If you ever chance to go there
You will never be the same.

Shining lights where lonely seamen
Whisper lies to lissom girls
Far less light where lonely people
Watch the dragon's tail uncurl
Chase the dragon, chase the dragon
Is the whisper in the night
Use the pipe or use the needle
Either one will make it right
I can love you, I will help you
Put your head upon my breast
Dream your dream, you foolish traveller
I will give your body rest.

In the streets the children suffer
From the doorways eyes are sad
Asking questions, needing answers
Is it good or is it bad?
I can't love you, I can't help you
I can't offer you parole
I am just a foolish traveller
And your mother owns my soul.

She of plastic, she of neon
She with eyes as black as night
She of artificial feelings
In the artificial light
She'll delight you she'll excite you
Force your soul to take a chance
Then with golden arms enfold you
In a never ending dance.

From an Armchair, 1997

There's a city up in Asia
Nestled in the China Sea
T'was the mother of all misfits
And a port for refugees
Still known as Fragrant Harbour
But these days it's not the same
If you ever say you lived there
Doubtless you'll be held to blame.

Soldiers from the middle kingdom
Slowly learning how to hate
Games of joy. And understanding
They cannot participate
Stay within their stony fortress
Watching through the iron gates
Sad they cannot join their brothers
They are prisoners of the state.

Fireworks defy a rain storm
Army trucks defy the mud
History's defining moments
When the tide is at its flood
Leave nine dragons dark and silent
Weeping for their fragrant one
Foetally she curls beneath them
In the shadows of the guns.

There's a city up in Asia
Nestled in the China Sea
And it seems so far away now
Just a faded memory
I knew the fragrance of its harbour
And the beauty of its song
I truly loved the happy people
Of the city called 'Heung Gong'.

Midnight,
30 June 1997

Sillyosophy

A Lunatic's Answer

I looked at the moon in the dark sky tonight
And wondered it if could see me
An insignificant dot on a planet
It gravitates round endlessly.

And I mused that the sun is an inconsequential
Part of the Milky Way
Which in turn is a trivial scene in Act One
Of a gigantic cosmic play.

Then I started to wonder, as most people do
If it goes on forever and ever
Or does something fit round it, or in it, or on it
That clenches the whole thing together?

I got to the point where the very idea
Was starting to make me feel dizzy
You know, when you think maybe there is a God
But if there's a God then where is He?

Oops I said 'He' when I should have said 'She'
'Cause I don't think a bloke's got the brains
To make heaven and hell and the cosmos as well
Let alone come in out of the rain.

And if She's around then She ought to come clean
And tell us how She got it started
And what's whizzing where, and what for, and is there
A place for our dearly departed?

Scientists declare there's no thing anywhere
That started as nothing at all
Except our universe and that is perverse
And it shows that they know bugger all.

'It went bang,' they all say in that know-it-all way
Now what sort of answer is that?
That's like saying hey, now you've stripped it away
You can put the skin back on the cat!

Was it the 'Big Bang' that started it all?
The theory's got quite a few backers
Some people say it was brought in to play
By one of the Murdochs or Packers.

Then I twigged as I looked at the moon all aglow
And the answer grabbed me by the knackers
It was God all alone in the dark long ago
Mischievously setting off crackers.

The Nerve of a Tree!

Look at me, said a tree that was standing by me
Do you know, since the day of my birth
I've been locked in one place and it's such a disgrace
For there's so much to see on this earth.

There are so many places and races I'd see
If I were a biped like you
I'd try Spain and Peru or North Kathmandu
But over that hill would do.

I'd go to Oslo and Holland, you know
And perhaps see a person in clogs
Just standing here it becomes rather drear
Then add to that, visits by dogs . . .

You bloody ingrate, I cried out, most irate
Your suggestion is simply absurd
You're just a tree, if we let you roam free
Next thing you'll want wings like a bird.

You can't defy Nature, it has legislature
In place to thwart flora of your size
You'll get hit by lightning if you go round frightening
People whilst anthropomorphised.

We cannot have trees wandering just as they please
You wait here while I go to town
I realised the danger and sought out a ranger
Who went out and chopped the tree down.

Bridges

Looking back down the road that my life has passed over
At all the tomorrows become yesterdays
Each day had a bridge where I knew joy or sorrow
Was hated or wanted but chose not to stay.

Leaving each part of my life for another
I always walked upright and looked down the track
And though sometimes foolish as I crossed those bridges
This wisdom I gathered, you cannot go back.

Bridges for burning, bridges for learning
Bridges for turning the heart from the knife
Bridges of sorrow and hope for tomorrow
And so I keep crossing the bridges of life.

Memories stir me from morning to madness
Of bridges I crossed that were tumbling down
I hurry from faces that haunt the dark places
Still deep in my mind they stay spinning around.

Music stirs memories of warm summer evenings
When I danced with a girl on the bridges of youth
I clung to her tightly and let her delight me
She took me from there to the bridges of truth.

When crossing the bridge of the heart I surrendered
Struck down by a feeling that I'd never known
For one shining hour I drowned in its power
But it faded and died and I walked on alone.

Some bridges I borrowed from people I'd followed
Travellers so weary they'd stopped by the way
Some others I shared with the people who cared
And the scared who stood trembling on feet made of clay.

I finally came to the bridges of wisdom
But although I searched, there was nothing to see
I'd walked all that way looking forward to answers
When all through my life they'd been following me.

Tonight I will sleep in the forest of ardour
And dream of lost chances and battles and shame
And wish back the day on the bridges of triumph
Where I held for one moment the bright light of fame.

Drift then my thoughts to the bridges of honour
Where memories of you are the ones that remain
It was there I found dignity, trust and devotion
As we whispered 'I love you' again and again.

In my final bright fancy a warmth will surround me
And thoughts of my crossing will call me away
To the last of the bridges I have to cross over
And cross it I must for there's no other way.

Bridges for burning, bridges for learning
Bridges for turning the heart from the knife
Bridges for sorrow and hope for tomorrow
And so I keep crossing the bridges of life.